I0410555

Special thanks to:

My parents,

for the motivation to succeed;

My teachers from pre-k to High School;

for helping me to understand the ABC's of life;

and the young people

who question the motives

and actions of humanity every day.

Introduction

This book is a collection of essays on varying topics, ranging from John Steinbeck's *Of Mice and Men* and his portrayal of the Great Depression, the impacts of childhood obesity, the need for confidence in black girls, how Haiti can turn its economic situation around, gun control, and the impacts of terrorist groups on children. These are My Thoughts on Social Issues and I will continue to shape them in the years to come because I believe children today are tomorrow's adults, and having a say in what is happening now will empower them to continue in the right path, while avoiding making the same mistakes. Each topic comes with citations to give the reader a variety of resources to explore. This book is mostly a compilation of all the essays that I have done in school, at Global High, Waxahachie, Texas. Sometimes, our best works are the ones we have done early in life. My Thoughts on Social Issues is also an invitation to motivate teens to express themselves on different social topics of their interests.

Table of Contents

Chapter 1

Hidden in Beauty

Poem to introduce "Kite yo Travay"

Crowds of people in the sweltering heat

A slight breeze as they overtake the streets

Brown skin glinting

As they

Yell and sell in makeshifts stands

Roasted peanuts, mangoes, meat patties,

And ice cold drinks, sticky coconut treats

As they

Coax frantic tourists to buy a colorful carved

souvenir

Amidst the cars growling over bumpy, dusty roads

Passing vibrant houses, some wobbly

Some strong in concrete block

Schoolchildren in crisp uniforms

Girls chattering, braids swinging

Women walking with jugs on their head,

The rolling hills and swaying trees in the

background

Toddlers chasing each other, chewing on sugarcane

Yes it's overwhelming, but delightfully so

As one

wades in the shapeless water

As one

Stops in the chaotic traffic at the "Neg Mawon"

statue

As he

Blows his conch shell for freedom.

This is Haiti, hidden in beauty

Chapter 2

"Kite yo Travay"

Let them Work

Natural disasters, political turmoil, and economic difficulties have been the setbacks of Haiti for decades. Naturally, when a third world country goes through a crisis, organizations swoop in attempting to save the day. Armed with eager volunteers and a surplus of supplies, the work done does typically aid the country. But, there is such a factor as excess assistance. Haiti has become extremely dependent on outside aid, without substantial results. In order for Haiti to become more self-sufficient, there should be less non-governmental organizations simply aiding, and a stronger focus on creating jobs and the long- term growth of their economy.

Haiti has gone through a great deal of instability, both natural disasters and government feuds. One of the most catastrophic events that ever impacted the island was the 2010 earthquake with a 7.0 magnitude on the Richter scale. There were about 230,000 people killed and over 300,000 that were injured (Estupiñán-Day, Saskia, Lafontant, and Acuña). Almost always the primary sector affected for any natural disaster, especially one of these sizes, is the health system. Although many medical organizations did step in to aid, most left as fast as they came. But, one of the medical organizations that made an impact in Haiti is PAHO (Pan American Health Organization). They did not just attempt to put a bandage on the medical system in times of crisis, but to heal it for the future. They focused on lasting health facilities, along with the distribution of needed medicine. PAHO not only aided but worked alongside Haitians, training locals in oral health and teaching them to become dentists through the Oral Health of Haiti Coalition, or OHOH (Estupiñán-Day, Saskia, Lafontant, and Acuña). This type of organization is not the problem, because they are trying to make lasting effects that will continue long after they have left.

The main target of what is wrong with most NGOs (non-governmental organizations), is the money and what it is being used for. Billions of dollars of aid was given to assist in the reconstruction of Haiti after the earthquake, and then soon after a flood. This was mainly controlled by private NGOs. ProPublica, a non-profit newsroom, investigated and found an answer as to what was happening with the money. They found that the Red Cross had raised half a billion dollars, but built only six homes. ProPublica hired people in charge of building the homes and overseeing them from other countries, rather than from Haiti. Those who were local Haitians had only received a fraction of the payment that the expatriates had received. The International organizations that are in Haiti to "help," often spend a *lot* of aid and money on overhead that doesn't go toward helping anyone (Baptiste). In other words, the people responsible for reviving the country are often times corrupted. Even when the money actually went towards aiding Haitians, the funds weren't used in the most efficient way.

A cholera epidemic began in October 2010, and infected nearly half a million Haitians within the first year (Klarrech and Polman). Water was the main reason why the disease spread so fast. But instead of putting the money into creating access to water for more Haitians, UNICEF and other NGOs decided that an awareness campaign on good hygiene was where the money should go. Ignoring their own message, they sent Haitians who lost their homes in the earthquake, to areas without showers or hand-washing stations. Considering that the people of Haiti would have helped in contributing ideas/places/etc. as to where the aid should go and there is no rationale as to why they weren't included in the discussion that would ultimately affect them. There are those who would then say, "Just forget organizations. Just bring jobs to the Haitians, brought by international corporations." This in turn creates another problem.

Producing jobs for Haitians is a huge part of the solution, but only if done in the right way. The Chancerelles Inc, a garment company in the US, is an example of how corporations can bring Haiti further into an economic crisis. There, bras and underpants are made for Elsie Undergarments in Florida. The price of a bra is set at $4.99. But, for such a cheap bra, there has to be a catch. The Haitian workers are offsetting the price of these cheap garments. The plant manager states, "We treat our workers like brothers and sisters" (Hoffmann). But the factory has little ventilation and outdated machines and the workers are getting paid between $1.16 and $1.89 per day. The National Labor Committee's report claims that well-known U.S. corporations--Kmart, Wal-Mart, J.C. Penney, and Sears--carry products assembled in Haiti for less than the minimum wage (Hoffmann). This seems to be a well-kept secret among the thousands of women who patron these stores, squealing over an attractive top at a very attractive price, unaware of the consequences of their latest find. After this depressing bit of information, it would seem that there is no way that Haiti can advance with only sweatshops or greedy NGOs as an option.

The Rhum Barbancourt factory, created and made in Haiti since 1862, is proof that there can be balance between aid and producing jobs with good pay. The 250 employees are all local Haitians and are paid 50 percent more than minimum wage of 5 dollars per day (Korten). But it is not just about working. The factory has also made a considerable impact on the neighboring people by creating a community center and soccer field. The long-term effects of not just a reasonable pay but the community impact, is why Rhum Barbancourt is a leading example of how a factory can be a positive advancement for Haiti.

Even when an organization isn't corrupt and has good intentions, an overabundance of aid can still be disastrous. Agriculture is a major industry in Haiti, and the free or inexpensive grain that was given to Haiti caused the Haitian farmers to suffer greatly. Without people needing the grain from their crops, there was no profit coming in. In March 2010, President Preval of Haiti called on the United States to "stop sending food aid" to Haiti, "so that our economy can recover and create jobs" (Ives). At the March 31 "International Donors Conference towards a New Future for Haiti" at the UN headquarters in New York, it was realized that agriculture was essential to Haiti's reconstruction."

Agriculture, perhaps more than other sector, is seen as essential to the country's health. Haitian journalist Michèle Montas said, "and the prevailing sentiment is that the peasantry has been neglected" (Ives). That conference's goal also showed that for an economy to move forward, the mistakes of the past have to retreat from the shadows and be revealed for all to see. This is no different for Haiti, and on March 10 Bill Clinton, the UN special envoy for Haiti, testified before the Senate Foreign Relations Committee because he led the move to make cuts in Haitian tariffs in the 1990s that ruined the country's rice industry. "We should have continued to work to help them be self-sufficient in agriculture" (Ives). One of Clinton's ideas on revitalizing Haiti is for 25,000 farmers to grow mangoes for Coca-Cola for a new Odwalla brand beverage. But, the debate is still heated as to whether factories are still the way to go due to fear of sweatshops. It shouldn't have to be one way or the other. The right type of factories and agriculture can live in harmony. Rum Barbancourt has proved this by using Haiti's sugarcane to produce rum in their factories.

Besides factories and agriculture, tourism is an industry that Haiti is trying to integrate itself into once again. The neighboring Caribbean islands with whom Haiti shares its island, such as Jamaica, Puerto Rico, and the Dominican Republic that took its independence from Haiti in 1848; they all have thousands of tourists each year, giving many locals jobs in hotels, restaurants, and tourist attractions. Haiti is already located in an area where tourism is prominent. Many wonder why tourism should continue in a place with demolished buildings and death. Writing in Britain's Independent newspaper, Senior Travel Editor Simon Calder asked, "In a part of the world that has fallen victim to a humanitarian disaster, should the very notion of tourism be abhorrent" (Springer)? Royal Caribbean cruises resumed traveling to Labadee, Haiti after the earthquake. An increased focus on tourism would be a strong way to spur economic growth.

As Haitians would say, "dèyè mòn gen plis mòn" (behind mountains, there are more mountains), and even with this strategy for an improved country, there will still be seemingly insurmountable struggles. The difference will be that the NGOs will not be causing them. With all achievements, there have to be times of setbacks.

But, when the local people get involved, they will learn by solving it together and not relying so much on outside help for their problems. The stakes are higher for them anyway. The people of Haiti care more about each other; what happens to their children's children, their country, and their economy. They care more than an outside foreigner, hired by the Red Cross ever would. They care more than a factory owner that oversees the production of undergarments ever would. Of course, no one learns to do anything by themselves, without being taught. So for the few and far between organizations that do care about what happens to a country once they leave, "Kite Ayisyen yo travay" (Let the Haitians work). Hire them to oversee the building of the homes that their people will benefit from. Let them be a part of where the money goes and how it is used. In the factories, let them work in good working conditions, no sweatshops or below the minimum wage pay. Use their agriculture, which benefits farmers, to produce goods and products. Admit to the mistakes that happened, because it does not matter how many new strategies someone comes up with. Without knowing where things went wrong, the same setbacks will occur again since nothing was solved in previous attempts. In the near future, if all who are part of changing the course of Haiti heed these words, the country will be able to stand on its own two feet, even better than before.

Works Cited

Baptiste, Nathalie. "Are Foreign NGOs Rebuilding Haiti or Just Cashing In?" Truthout. Web. 4 Oct. 2015.

Estupiñán-Day, Saskia, Christina Lafontant, and Acuña Maria Cecilia. "Integrating Oral Health Into Haiti's National Health Plan: From Disaster Relief to Sustainable Development." *PanAmerican Journal Of Public Health* 30.5 (2011): 484-489. *Academic Search Complete*. Web. 17 Sept. 2015.

Hoffmann, Marcelo. "Sweatshop Haiti." Progressive 60.12 (1996): 15. Academic Search Complete. Web. 4 Oct. 2015.

Ives, Kim. "Haiti Reconstruction: Factories, Not Fields." NACLA Report On The Americas 43.3 (2010): 4-5. Academic Search Complete. Web. 20 Sept. 2015.

Klarreich, Kathie and Polman, Linda. "The NGO Republic of Haiti." The Nation. 31 Oct. 2012. Web. 4 Oct. 2015.

Korten, Tristram. "Rum And Hope." Atlantic 305.4 (2010): 19-20. Academic Search Complete. Web. 20 Sept. 2015.

"PAHO Works To Restore Public Health Services In Haiti." *Bulletin Of The World Health Organization* 82.4 (2004): 316-317. *Academic Search Complete*. Web. 17 Sept. 2015.

Springer, Bevan. "Tourism can help Haiti recover." New York Amsterdam News 21 Jan. 2010: 14. Academic Search Complete. Web. 20 Sept. 2015.

Chapter 3

Give me Junk Food or Give me Death: Preventing Childhood Obesity in America

A pediatrician specializes in the health of the youth under the age of 21, focusing on their development and the prevention of illnesses whether minor or serious. However, over the past decades, obesity in children has become an issue that continues to magnify and can no longer be ignored. One cannot solve a dilemma this severe by simply slapping on a band aid, prescribing antibiotics, and handing a child a lollipop with a smile. Childhood obesity has more than doubled in children and quadrupled in adolescents over the past thirty years in the United States (Orenstein). There needs to be a new solution in preventing this, because the barely existent solutions are obviously not working. The solution should be in a place where children populate almost every day, and a set of daily structure is already in place: schools. This is where the problem ends, and the solution begins. In order to prevent childhood obesity in America, schools must take a greater initiative to integrate healthy lifestyle choices into their students.

Awareness has been spread on obesity, and how children need to learn how to be healthy, but the negative effects haven't always been clear, with confusion as to where the line is drawn between being overweight and obese. Overweight is the accumulation of excess body weight for a particular height from fat, muscle, bone, and/or water. Obesity is having excess body fat (Center for Disease

Control and Prevention). However, over time being overweight can lead to becoming obese. When a negative habit continues, it becomes worse without a change in lifestyle. There are cases in which previous health problems results in the precedent to an unhealthy body weight, however as of 2012 one third of children and adolescents are obese (Orenstein). This extreme increase cannot all be explained by previous health conditions or genetics. There are not only temporary effects, but long term effects caused by obesity in children. A higher risk of prediabetes, bone and joint problems, sleep apnea, has psychological effects such as a low-self-esteem (Center for Disease Control and Prevention). Future long-term effects include obese children becoming obese adults. Adult health problems of heart disease, type 2 diabetes, stroke, cancer in the breast, colon, kidney, among other areas, and osteoarthritis have an increased chance of forming in an obese person (Center for Disease Control and Prevention). Besides the physical health effects, one often ignored are the psychological effects of children dealing with obesity, or who are even overweight. In a society that puts a premium on thinness, studies show that children as young as 6 years may associate negative stereotypes with excess weight and believe that a heavy child is simply less likable (American Academy of Pediatrics). An obese child has a high risk of being bullied at school, and becoming depressed, and feeling lonely. Some overweight children like these might seek emotional comfort in food, adding even more calories to their plates (American Academy of Pediatrics). B y being obese, the emotional stress can cause them to continue to eat, and in turn can lead to more health problems. The present generation should not die younger than the past. That is the road we are heading for if nothing is changed about the health lifestyle habits in America.

Convenient access to unhealthy foods and less exercising has caused this increase in obesity rates. With fast food chains lining up streets, their signs advertising cheap, greasy food, in close proximity to neighborhoods, families now more than ever frequent these establishments. Since 1970, the amount of fast food restaurants in business doubled, which equates to about 300,000 establishments in the United States (Muntel). At this same time, obesity rates in children began to grow. The general caloric recommendation for Americans is 1,500-1,800 calories per-day and around 50-60 grams of total fat (Muntel). In just one meal at a fast food restaurant, a person can exceed the amount of calories to eat. Less people are making home cooked meals at home, and instead of going out more often. It's cheaper and fills them up, so do not see the problem with their actions. The College of William and Mary conducted a study on a sample of elementary and middle school students and their proximity to fast food chains, and the correlation with their body max index (measure of body fat based on height and weight), keeping their socioeconomic status in mind. The results showed that students residing within one-tenth or one-quarter of a mile from a fast food restaurant had significantly higher BMI's than those who did not (Mellor, Dolan, and Rapoport). These were not full service restaurants, (restaurants that cook most of the food themselves). It was the high caloric intake and sugar of fast food restaurants that caused the BMI increases, not merely just because families were eating out. As well as fast food chains being so close to home, so are schools. It may not be possible to prevent the access of fast food so close to neighborhoods, schools can counteract the effect. It can be a place where children learn healthy lifestyle choices, and help them once they leave the front doors, and are bombarded with unhealthy choices.

As well as fast-food being a contributing factor to childhood obesity, the increase of excess sugar in food products is partially to blame as well. High fructose syrup was introduced in the 1970's due to the low cost and has replaced other types of sweeteners in foods that are processed. HFCS, (High fructose corn syrup), is found in breakfast cereals, beverages, breads, snack foods, and desserts (R. E. Morgan). The consumption of soft drinks has had a 123% increase between the 1970's and 1980's, with HFCS as the main sweetener (R. E. Morgan). The International Association for the Study of Obesity claimed that there was inconclusive evidence on whether HFCS increases obesity. However, when the consumption of soft drinks increased, the milk consumption in children decreased (R.E. Morgan). So when given so many unhealthy, sugary choice, children will choose the sweets instead of protein, such as milk. Losing key nutrients and replacing those with empty calories does lead to obesity. If children have such a wide accessibility to sugar in everything they eat, they won't be able to learn and explore other healthier options, except in school.

One could then argue, instead of schools, educate parents on healthy choices, and they will in turn educate their children. After all, they purchase the groceries, they cook the food, they drive the car into a drive-in, and they can choose to take them out to ride their bike or go to a park. But, parents cannot be trusted to keep those choices taught to them. Many times, obese children tend to have obese parents. Often, it is hard for them to even control what they eat and if they exercise. This isn't to say, parents are completely at blame, however if they are going through their own difficulties with their health mindset, then they most likely will not be able to help their children. Someone one else has to step in. A qualitative study conducted by the

International Journal of Behavioral Nutrition and Physical Activity took a group of 18 obese children, ages around ten, and 24 parents, who were expected to lose weight by being physically active and eating healthy (Schalkwijk). The parents struggled to adopt the new rules, and children suffered from inconsistent parenting. However, if children had outside support from schools, it would bring the structure needed to be exposed to a healthy lifestyle.

Another area that children have gained extreme easy access to, and gives no support for healthy choices is the media. Advertising has a huge influence on children and adolescents. Young people view more than 40,000 ads per year on television alone (Jain). The internet has also contributed to advertisements. So many sugary-processed foods either have a friendly mascot, comes with a toy inside, or a catchy tune. It's integrating negative choices into their minds. It is not about enjoying not-so healthy foods sparingly anymore, but yanking their mothers' sleeves as they point to their favorite sugary cereal brand or sneaking bags of chips into the cart. However, students as well as being succumbed to the media, spend about 8 hours of their day in a school. Schools can counteract the negative media by introducing them to a different mindset on junk foods.

It seems that everywhere one looks, children are being swept into negative healthy choices in their environments. Schools are the only options that could have set rules and could make an impact on preventing obesity in their students. It could be argued that there is no way to accomplish this huge goal, but sometimes it's not taking huge, drastic measures, but small steps that lead to significant results in the future. A study conducted on high schools in the Netherlands examined 3 strategies for promoting the sale of lower-calorie food products from vending machines in high schools (Kocken). Increasing the availability of lower-calorie products in vending machines did not have a drop in sales, and the students were able to make healthier choices. School lunches are also a way to make an impact on students. In Pennsylvania, a study was done in an elementary school during 1 week each year for 7 years. It was conducted in a town that contained mostly poor, and obese children. There were healthier menu choices and foods with high calories and a low nutrition decreased from 22% in 2005 go 0% in 2011 (Cluss, Fee, Culyba, Bhat, and

Owen). There was no significant decline in the percentage of children who purchased cafeteria lunches. However, some school lunch supporters say that there doesn't need to be a change, and that school lunch programs meet the U.S. Department of Agriculture guidelines, that no more that 30 percent of calories can be from fat, and less that 10 percent can come from saturated fat (Food Fight! Should School Lunches Be Healthier?) However in a lunch line, there is the main meal a student can consume for that day, as well as foods that are offered every day, such as slices of cheese pizza, or soft pretzels. Many students eat a slice of pizza for lunch continuously, because that option is provided to them all the time. A large amount of them does not eat the meal that includes the protein and vegetables that meet the guidelines. Then there is controversy as to where a school, such as one that is in a poor rural community, will get the funds to switch to healthier meal choices. There should be a focus on getting funds for school lunch programs, as much as there is for sports or other extracurricular activities. The Pew Charitable Trusts and the Robert Wood Johnson Foundation recently released a report showing that 88% of school districts need at least one piece of kitchen equipment and 50% need infrastructure changes in order to provide healthier meals (Sifferlin). Funding should go to improving this, and getting proper equipment to slice fresh fruit and vegetables, as well as storage for fresh food.

Healthier school lunches also bring the question as to how children who do not have enough money for lunch would eat. Along with their socioeconomic status, the race of a child also has significant, but different rates of obesity growth percentage. African Americans, Native Americans, and Mexican Americans, all had higher rates of obesity in children than any other racial groups (Caprio, Daniels, Drewnowski, Kaufman, Palinkas, Rosenbloom, and Schwimmer). The lifestyle of a child's home is characterized by their culture. It's not possible, and unethically senseless to call social services on a family simply because their traditional meals aren't always healthy, but that still does not bring an answer on how to slow the growing rates of obesity. The Centers for Disease Control reported that in 2000 the prevalence of obesity was 19% of non-Hispanic black children and 20% of Mexican American children, compared with 11% of non-Hispanic white children (Caprio, Daniels,

Drewnowski, Kaufman, Palinkas, Rosenbloom, and
Schwimmer). The one place where one could
usually find multiple races together, or at the least
majority of the same race together, is in schools.
 Giving them an education in an environment that is
different from their usual ones, as well as free of
cultural preferences, can open their eyes. If they
have an inability to purchase their lunch, just as
many schools have free and reduced lunch
programs; this would be in place as well during the
transition to healthier foods.

The first lady, Michelle Obama began a
"Let's Move" initiative to provide better nutrition at
schools in America. It is the first major revision to
school meal standards in 15 years (Let's Move).
There are also more whole grains, fruits, and
vegetables, as well as low-fat milk dairy products,

and less sodium and fat. There is also a greater
focus on portion size control, designed differently
for each grade level.

Besides food consumption, physical activity
has also lost its importance in school systems. At
home, it is less physical activity, and more
computers and video games. A survey showed that
that 74% of children between the ages of 5 and 10
do not get enough exercise on a daily basis, based
on the 60 minutes of daily **physical**
activity recommended in the government's Physical
Activity Guidelines for American Heart Foundation
(Hendrick). The survey found that 52% of parents
said they'd been forced to cut back, on their
children's after-school activities, because they could
not afford the cost (Hendrick). But PE is free,
because it is a class. Students can benefit from

physical fitness, and it is at no cost. In California, their education code requires their students in grades 1-6 to receive at least 200 minutes of physical education per 10 school days. In grades 7 to 12, it is 400 minutes per 10 days (LaFee). However, 48 percent of the elementary schools and 23 percent of middle schools and high schools did not meet the standards (LaFee). Budget cuts are usually first made to programs such as PE. Schools focus on anti-drugs, and academic excellence, but they should also focus on their students being healthy, because it might be the only place where that can become a focus.

To become healthy, children have to be in an environment that only has access to a healthy mindset. After all, humans are a product of their environment. What they see is what they will do.

Therefore, if all they see is their parents taking them to fast food chains lit up at night, and a choice of watching TV rather than riding their bike, that is all they will become and all their children will become. So if we want obesity in children to end, we have to show them how to end it. Ending childhood obesity will start in a school, because at a school one learns. The students will learn how to save themselves.

Works Cited

Alexandra, Sifferlin. "USDA Grants Help

Schools Serve Healthier Lunches" Time Magazine.

18 April. 2014. *Academic Search Complete* . Web

27 Nov. 2015.

American Academy of Pediatrics. "The

Emotional Toll of Obesity." 21 Nov. 2015. Web. 27

Nov. 2015.

Center for Disease Control and Prevention,

"Childhood Obesity Facts." 27 Aug. 15. Web. 5

Nov. 2015.

Cluss, PA., Fee L., Culyba RJ., Bhat KB,

and Owen K. "Effect of Food Service

Nutrition Improvements on ElementarySchool

Cafeteria Lunch Purchase Patterns." *US National

Library of Medicine National Institute of Health*

84.6 (2014): 355-62. *Academic Search Complete.*
Web. 27 Nov. 2015.

"Food Fight! Should School Lunches Be
Healthier?." *Current Events* 105.19 (2006):
3. *Academic Search Complete.* Web. 24 Nov.
2015.

Hendrick, Bill. "Most Young Kids Don't Get
Enough Exercise." *WebMD.* 11 April. 2011.
Web. 27 Nov.2015.

Jain, Anjali. "Temptations In Cyberspace:
New Battlefields In Childhood Obesity." *Health
Affairs* 29.3 (2010): 425-429. *Academic Search
Complete.* Web. 4 Nov. 2015.

Kocken, Paul L., et al. "Promoting The
Purchase
Of Low-Calorie Foods From School Vending
Machines: A Cluster-Randomized Controlled

Study." Journal Of School Health 82.3 (2012):

115-122. *Academic Search Complete.* Web. 6 Nov.

2015.

LaFee, Scott. "Let's Get Physical! P.E.

Struggles To Make The Grade." *Education*

Digest 73.6 (2008): 49-52. *Academic Search*

Complete. Web. 24 Nov. 2015.

"Let's Move." *Healthy Schools*. Web. 27

Nov. 2015.

Mellor, Jennifer M., Carrie B. Dolan, and

Ronald B. Rapoport. "Child Body Mass

Index, Obesity, and Proximity To Fast

Food Restaurants." *International Journal*

Of Pediatric Obesity 6.1 (2011):

60-68. *Academic Search Complete*. Web. 4

Nov. 2015.

Morgan, R. E. "Does Consumption Of High-Fructose Corn Syrup Beverages Cause Obesity In Children?." *Pediatric Obesity* 8.4 (2013): 249-254. *Academic Search Complete*. Web. 4 Nov. 2015.

Peggy, Orenstein. "The Fat Trap." *New York Times Magazine*(2010): 15. *Academic Search Complete*. Web. 4 Nov. 2015.

Sarah, Muntel. "Obesity Action Coalition » Fast Food – Is It the Enemy?" *Obesity Action Coalition Fast Food Is It the Enemy Comments*. Web. 27 Nov. 2015.

Schalkwijk, A. A. H., et al. "Perspectives Of Obese Children And Their Parents On Lifestyle Behavior Change: A Qualitative Study." *International Journal Of Behavioral*

Nutrition & Physical Activity 12.1 (2015): 1-
8. *Academic Search Complete*. Web. 4 Nov. 2015

Sonia Caprio., **Stephen R. Daniels.**, **Adam**
Drewnowski., Francine R. Kaufman., Lawrence A.
Palinkas., Arlan L. Rosenbloom, and **Jeffrey B.**
Schwimmer . "Childhood Obesity: Implications for
Prevention and Treatment." *US National Library of*
Medicine National Institutes of Health (2008):
2211-2221. Web. 27 Nov. 2015.

Chapter 4

In Guns We Trust

The average bullet travels around 2,500 feet per second (Mythbusters). In that second, someone has the power to control a weapon and impact its target. The right for that power comes from the Constitution, founded by the country's leaders when America was just beginning to stand on its wobbly legs. As gun violence continues to be a present issue, the Second Amendment's true meaning of the right to bear arms remains a controversy. However, to interpret the historical stance on gun control, one must go back to where it all began.

The gun's first appearance in America was brought by pilgrims in the New World, mainly used for hunting (Fisanick 14). In the 1800s, small arms would become more affordable and accessible to people, meaning that laws for gun safety began. The first type of gun control can be traced back to ownership cards, and they would increase after significant wars in a country (Fisanick 14). Ratified in 1791, the Second Amendment reassured the rights of American citizens to bear arms. How this applies to guns in the 21st century is the real question. David Burton, author of *The Second Amendment*, argues that the founding fathers set this amendment in place for all citizens to have guns to defend themselves, as well as the right to own tanks and fighter jets (Mantyla). Burton, like many others, twisted the Second Amendment to what he wanted to hear.

Unlike the early pilgrims, 48% of gun owners say that their primary reason for having a gun now is for protection, 32% say they have a gun primarily for hunting, and a small amount for other reasons, like target shooting (Pew Research Center). Amidst the current highlights on gun shootings, gun owners fear what this might mean for their freedom. The Second Amendment's exact words state that, "A well-regulated militia being necessary to the security of a free State, the right of the People to keep and bear arms shall not be infringed." Those who are pro-gun control stated that "a well-regulated militia" really meant the National Guard and the state's rights to preserve the guard. This was their personal take on the meaning. However, long before the Constitution was made, European political writers used the term "well-regulated militia" when pertaining to all individuals, armed with their own weapons, including firearms, and founding fathers such as George Mason and Richard Henry Lee later interpreted it the same way (Institute for Legislative Action). This meaning in historical terms reveals the truth of the phrase.

The government has also contemplated what the forefathers were trying to say. In a critical case, District of Columbia V. Heller, Dick Heller was a police officer which permitted him to have a gun. He also wanted to keep a gun in his own home, but was not allowed the license he applied for. He then complained to his district court that it was against his rights by the Second Amendment. The court ruled 5 to 4 that the prevention of firearms for protection was against the Constitution (Chicago-Kent College of Law at Illinois Tech).

The Second Amendment was in America's best interest. It was never intended for guns to be in

the hands of people who were not capable of
controlling them, or who would harm others by
using their rights as a loophole. James Madison,
author of the Constitution, wrote the Federalist
Paper number 46 in 1788 stating, "Americans have
"the advantage of being armed"- unlike the citizens
of other countries where "the governments are
afraid to trust the people with arms (Straub). The
freedom of the people to use guns, according to the
forefathers, should not be compromised by other's
lack of ability to use that right responsibly.

Works Cited

Chicago-Kent College of Law at Illinois Tech."District of Columbia v. Heller." *Oyez.* Illinois Institute of Technology, n.d. Web. 17 Feb. 2016.

Fisanick, Christina. *Gun Control.* Michigan: Greenhaven Press, 2010. Print.

Institute for Legislative Action. "Second Amendment." *NRA-ILA.* National Rifle Association, n.d. Web. 17 Feb. 2016.

Mantyla, Kyle. "Barton: Second Amendment Guarantees an Individual Right to Own A Tank or Fighter Jet." *Right Wing Watch.* People For the American Way, 26 Sep. 2013. Web. 17 Feb. 2016.

Mythbusters. "Dodge A Bullet." *Mythbusters the Exhibition.* Discovery Communications, LLC, n.d. Web. 18 Feb. 2016

Pew Research Center. "Why Own a Gun? Protection Is Now Top Reason." *U.S. Politics & Policy.* People-Press, 12 Mar. 2013. Web. 17 Feb. 2016.

Straub, Steve. "Federalist Paper #46- The Influence of the State and Federal Governments Compared." *The Federalist Papers.* The Federalist Papers Project, n.d. Web. 17 Feb.2016.

"The Constitution of the United States," Amendment 2. 15 Dec. 1791.

Chapter 5

Dreams Not Yet Fulfilled

Only 1 in 3 Americans are truly happy (Gregoire). That may be the reason why inspirational posters about giving up on one's dreams clutter the walls of public places. People need to be reminded to believe in something at every step they make. Many face challenges that prevent them from ever getting the chance to reach their version of happy. As progressive as one wants to think America has always been, in the past so many people have felt discrimination of some kind, to include the mentally ill, women, African Americans, and the list goes on. These people' dreams were simple: to feel accepted and create their own happy place in the world. However, a lot of them stopped feeling like they could pursue their happiness. John Steinbeck's *Of Mice and Men* uses characters to illustrate the treatment of people in America who were disadvantaged during the 1930's.

The setting of this novel does not offer a cheeky story of flappers in sparkly fringe and suave men doing the Charleston on their way to the bank. The roaring 20s were over, and the Great Depression danced its way in instead. Beginning in 1929, the Great Depression caused over 13 million people to become unemployed and in need of work (History Channel). Ranch workers were also severely affected by this. Droughts caused by the Dust Bowl pushed many out of the South into plentiful fields in California (Horowitz). The main characters from the novel, George and Lennie, found themselves in Salinas Valley, North California. They were among the migrant workers searching for hope and dreams in a harsh reality. However, most of these men traveled by themselves. This was more practical since they continuously roamed from place to place. Others thought it was strange that George and Lennie were companions on the road including Slim, a fellow worker commenting, "Funny how you an' him string along together. You know how the hands are, they just come in and get their bunk and work a month, and then they quit and go out alone" (Steinbeck 39). What was even more uncommon than traveling together was the type of person George was traveling with. At first Lennie seems a bit dim, but one soon realizes that he is mentally challenged and not just an amusing character.

During the 30's, most of the mentally ill did not have a George looking out for them. From lack of finances, institutions where most of the mentally ill were sent became worse during the Great Depression. Many of the mentally ill ended up in hospitals, and they had to leave before getting treatment due to overcrowding (Freeman). Lennie might have gotten the seemingly magic cure of a lobotomy, a procedure done by going through the eye to damage the tissue in the brain, and this was thought to solve all the problems of the mentally ill (Freeman). Lennie was lucky and strong enough to be able to work, but one could argue that his mentality prevented him from seeing that his dream of having a piece of land with George was impossible due to their reality. After all, he could not even keep a steady job to fulfill what he wanted in his future, with the tendency of always getting into trouble by accident. Taking even more steps backward at their goal, George had to take them somewhere else due to Lennie's incident at the previous job: "Well, he seen this girl in a red dress. Dumb bastard like he is, he wants to touch ever'thing he likes.-He was so scared he wouldn't let go of that dress.-Well that girl rabbits in an' tells the law that she has been raped" (Steinbeck 41-42). Even though it frequently got him into trouble, his childlike manner allowed him to do what the other characters could not do: the ability to have an infinite hope in something.

Although stubbornly unwilling to admit that the dream of owning a piece of land was not just Lennie's but also his, George never fully believed that it would ever happen. This was shown when he spoke to Candy after Lennie accidentally killed Curley's wife. "I think I knowed from the very first. I think I knowed we'd never do her [the farm]. He usta like to hear about it so much I got to thinking maybe we would" (Steinbeck 94). He was also never able to admit to Lennie that he saw him as a friend, and not just a nuisance as he frequently loved to remind him. "God a'mighty, if I was alone, I could live so easily...you can't keep a job and you lose me every job I get (Steinbeck 11). But without that friendship, George could have easily ended up like the men who became so lonely; they turned to women to fill their voids.

Women were not thought of as equal to men, even while they had to support their families in ways never done before during the Great Depression, with some leaving housework and seeking income instead (National Women's History Museum). Many had to resort to prostitution as available jobs dwindled and they had to find a way to survive (Independence Hall Association). For lonely migrant workers on ranches, they were only thought of as a distraction and nothing more. Curley, the son of the ranch boss, was a jealous, short-tempered man who somehow got ahold of a wife (Cliffsnotes). Of course, being as important as he is, the reader only knows her as Curley's wife. As Curley liked to remind the isolated ranchers, it was his wife and not theirs. So they looked, but did not touch, reinforcing the idea of her being emotionless, conniving, and provocative. "She's a jail bait all set on the trigger ranch with a bunch of guys on it ain't no place for a girl, 'specially like her" (Steinbeck 51). But she became that person out of loneliness, yearning for someone other than the husband she settled for after giving up on her dream of becoming a star. As soon as she stopped believing, she went looking for trouble to take away the pain of feeling nothing. Curley's wife could never have a conversation with anyone until Lennie came into the picture. She took an interest in him, after Lennie had another "incident" and broke Curley's hand (Steinbeck 63). At first he was apprehensive, and Curley's wife reached her breaking point saying, "What's the matter with me? Ain't I got to talk to nobody? I ain't doing no harm to you" (Steinbeck 87-88). She proceeded to tell her life story of giving up on dreams to Lennie, the only one who would listen and that still believed in his.

Another person that Lennie was able to connect with when others could not was Crooks, an African American who took care of the horses on the ranch. The color of his skin made his experience on the ranch different from anyone else's. During the Great Depression, African Americans were the first to lose their jobs, including on ranches (The Gale Group). Crooks was lucky enough to have work when others of his race did not. But he was completely isolated from the other workers, and the degrading way they treated him was a common, everyday occurrence. Lennie came into his room to search for a puppy on the ranch that he had claimed as his own, and though Crooks's pride almost prevented him from staying in the room they were able to have a conversation (Steinbeck 68). The hatred for blacks during the time was shown as the workers repeatedly called Crooks a contemptuous term, nigger (Steinbeck 20). But simple minded Lennie, unaware of his role as a white male when conversing with Crooks, was able to connect with him in a matter of minutes when no one else would bother. Crooks commented on Lennie's relationship with George saying, "You got George. You know he's goin' to come back. S'pose you didn't have nobody. S'pose you couldn't go into the bunkhouse and play rummy 'cause you was black" (Steinbeck 71). Crooks had become so beaten down and put in his place that he had resigned himself to a fate where he would always be seen as inferior.

Lennie's death is tragically ironic by being foreshadowed by the death of a dog, what he loves the most, and his life is ended by whom he loves the most, George. George shoots Lennie after he gets into an altercation with Curley's wife during a conversation which led him to petting her hair and killing her in a state of mental panic when he was unable to let go (Steinbeck 91). George realized that there was no way to pull Lenny out of the mess he made, and decided to put him out of his misery just like that poor, old dog. However, Lennie never stopped believing in a world where he and George would have their dream. Like a little child constantly needing reassurance, George repeatedly was asked to tell him their future plans for a farm, "We'd jus' live there. We'd belong there. There wouldn't be no more running...we'd have our own place where we belonged and not sleep in no bunkhouse" (Steinbeck 57). Lennie died before seeing that dream come true, but the other characters in the novel had died long before he did.

They stopped believing in something that gave them a reason to want to push back with how the world viewed them during their time. They stopped believing in their hopes and wants. But simple-minded Lennie made an impact on them all, even amidst the unintentional misfortunes he caused. His childlike manner reminded the people at Salinas Valley ranch that it is okay to believe in something, no matter how futile, if it means that hope has not died in a person before they do.

Works Cited

Cliffsnotes. "Character List." *Of Mice and Men.* Houghton Mifflin Harcourt, n.d. Web. 9 Mar. 2016.

Freeman, Shanna. "Psychiatric Care in the 1930s: The Lobotomy's Origins." *How Lobotomies Work.* How Stuff Works, n.d. Web. 6 Mar. 2016.

Gregoire, Carolyn."Only 1 In 3 Americans Are Very Happy, According To Harris Poll." Huffpost Healthy Living. Huffington Post, 1 June 2013. Web. 6 Mar. 2016.

History Channel. "The Great Depression." *History.* A&E Television Networks, n.d. Web. 6 Mar. 2016.

Horowitz, Joanna. "Tensions on the Ranch." Seattle Repertory Theatre. Artsfund, n.d. Web. 9 Mar. 2016.

Independence Hall Association. "Social and Cultural Effects of the Depression." *Pre-Columbian to the New Millennium.* IHA, n.d. Web. 8 Mar. 2016.

National Women's History Museum. "The Depression and World War II." *A History of Women in Industry.* NWHM, n.d. Web. 8 Mar. 2016.

Steinbeck, John. *Of Mice and Men.* New York: Penguin Books, 1993. Print.

The Gale Group. "Black Americans 1929-1941." *Historic Events for Students: The Great Depression.* Cengage Learning, n.d. Web. 8 Mar. 2016.

Chapter 6

Terrorists in the Minds of the Young

Imagine two children. They get up in the morning, get dressed, go to school, and spend time with their family. One of them studies the Koran, and the other might study the Bible, or learn morals. Throughout their life, both children are taught by their religious leaders, or whoever has influence on their life. What is taught is reinforced at home. Now imagine this stereotype for how terrorism weeds its way into society dissipating into thin air. The events that surround the breeding ground for when terrorists' and victims' lives will tragically collide in the future are much more intricate than what is perceived. Terrorism is a word that no one likes talking about, but is no longer easy to avoid. People usually associate this word with adults. For most, an adult is mature enough to understand the implications of their actions. However, most who pledge their allegiance to terrorist groups are misled into believing false information, and undergo brainwashing. If someone at the age of supposed understanding is vulnerable to terrorism, a child's mind would be even easier to manipulate. There is argument that these children are not victims. What they have done is indisputably wrong, but they were blinded by false lies and promises at a young age. They are used by the people they look up to religiously. On the other spectrum, the victims who are targeted by the actions of the terrorist groups include children as well. Terrorist groups have an impact on the children who are coaxed into "fulfilling their destiny" and the victims who suffer the consequences of those who embark on a Jihad.

It is no longer necessary for children to be in the same country as their terrorist groups to be taught their beliefs. They can now be the target from across the world: online or onsite, as shown in Britain when three Muslim girls disappeared from their homes. Khadiza Sultana , Amira Abase, and Shamima Begum, ages ranging from 15 to 16, left their homes in London to join ISIS in Syria (Bennhold). As much as this is a shock to the world on how ISIS could have reached teenage girls from far distances, it comes at an even greater surprise to the people the girls interacted with, who did not even see it coming. To convince anyone to take such a drastic turn from their life, one would think that maybe the girls were rebellious already, and there might have been early signs of their allegiance with ISIS. However, this was the opposite. All three Muslim girls attended Bethnal Green Academy, and were known for their stellar grades and good behavior (Bennhold). Later on, there had been some signs of a difference in their actions, such as lower grades and missing assignments, but their family just thought it was teenagers being teenagers (Bennhold). It is easier to notice changes in an adult's behavior then it is in younger people, because it can appear as teenage rebellion, and not something more dangerous. The constant new girl-to-girl recruitment strategy is what reigned in any doubts the girls might have had of leaving (Bennhold). The girls took drastic actions to journey to Syria, becoming part of something they were led to believe. However, in other parts of the world, giving up one's life is the ultimate show of faith.

Recruiting adults is also different from recruiting children; because of the way they convince them to join their cause. They can no longer use the promise of an incredible afterlife, and result to bribes of a happy life and sweets to lure them in (Boghani). In Afghanistan, these tactics are becoming more and more common. In Afghanistan, boys primarily, see adult fighters in their communities (Boghani). Those are the only "role models" available, and naturally they end up wanting to be like them. What the ISIS recruiters have on their side is poverty. They come to the families, demanding money or a child (Boghani). Since they could never come up with that money, they have no choice but to give their children away.

These children are in the heart of terrorism recruiting, and it undoubtedly affects their future. However, the future of the children who are targets of terrorist attacks is altered as well. There is a huge focus on ISIS, but there are many other terrorist groups operating and affecting children and their families around the world. Boko Haram is a Nigerian based group that seeks to replace the current government with one based on Islamic principles (Counterterrorism Guide). They call themselves Group of the Sunni people for the Calling and Jihad; however the majority of the population knows them as Boko Haram, whose translation means Western education is forbidden (Counterterrorism Guide). For many children around the world, education is one of the only means in making a life for themselves that is better than what they're facing, but many terrorist groups, including Boko Haram, condemn it. Boko Haram proved its name true when in 2014; the terrorist group was brought to the world's center stage by abducting 200 girls from their boarding school in Nigeria (Abubakar). Following later in early March, the state government closed all of its 85 secondary schools and sent more than 120,000 students home following increasing Boko Haram attacks on schools (Abubakar). Before Boko Haram began its raid on schools in northeast Nigeria six years ago, the region recorded the lowest school enrollment rate in the country, especially for girls, as well as the lowest level of literacy and highest incidence of poverty. In 2014, over half a million children in northeast Nigeria have had to flee to safety in the past five months (Morgan). The fear of going to school, and never coming back home is now in the heart of many students, as well as their families.

The amount of school shootings have continued to be a cause for concern, but what parents also have to face is their children's safety by those who pledge their allegiance to terrorist groups. Innocent children not just in the country of the terrorist group's origin, but also abroad where further attacks are taken are now becoming casualties in the war on terror. On April 15, 2013, Dzhokhar A. Tsarnaev and Tamerlan Tsarnaev, created two pressure cooker bombs that exploded during the Boston Marathon, and a shootout then commenced (History.com Staff). Three people were killed, and over 260 people were injured. Out of the three killed, one was 8 year old Martin Richard

(Associated Press and Louise Boyle). A young boy, who had barely begun to experience life died, as a sacrifice to what the Tsarnaev brothers claimed their allegiance to that day. The one surviving terrorist, Dzhokhar Tsarnaev, was taken to trial for a verdict on the death penalty (Associated Press and Louise Boyle). David King, a veteran military combat surgeon, took to the stand and stated that Martin Richard experienced pain and bled to death (Associated Press and Louise Boyle). In a senseless act, he died with no comfort. Tsarnaev has been sentenced to death by the decision of the court in Boston (Winter). However, his death will never bring Martin Richard or any of the innocent dead back to life. Martin Richard should be a reminder of why being part of terrorism is never an honor, no matter the false belief that it is justified by religion.

The means for communication to a larger audience is one of the tactics of the terrorist groups. The internet has made it increasingly possible to coordinate and recruit people (Kaplan). The population that one can find frequenting the internet more than the rest is typically children. Terrorist groups are known for creating propaganda videos, as well as coordinating attacks via the internet (Kaplan). However, they have also found ways to use technology to get to children. Terrorist groups have created websites specifically for youth, with cartoons and games (Homeland Security Institute). What is even more surprising is that these sites are in English (Homeland Security Institute). The Palestinian group Hamas focuses on young children with its youth website, al-Fateh ("The Conqueror"). This includes characters similar to Disney, and games that promote violence and praise jihad (Homeland Security Institute). If terrorist groups are efficiently using the internet to broadcast their message, than those against terrorism need to advocate their message as well. For example, Singapore's Islamic Religious Council, (MUIS), has developed websites for youth, to include a site that responds to religious queries and a site devoted to rebutting extremist ideologies (Homeland Security Institute). Another solution, although controversial, is to block terrorist websites from the public. Some argue that this is a violation of the government by using censorship. However, there is no good that would come out of allowing terrorist groups access into what they need the most: the minds of people to agree to do their bidding. France has attempted to do this, although it's still in the works as of 2015, to block 5 websites that advocate terrorism (Greenwald). There is a delicate balance between government censorship and the safety of citizens. In this case, the balancing act is dangerously close to toppling over in favor of terrorism if something is not done.

Although the internet is used as mentioned beforehand, terrorists are recruiting through ways that are not immediately thought of when picturing their techniques. A documentary done by Real Stories in 2014 follows a young Muslim woman named Aisha who is set on finding how other women are being recruited by terrorist such as ISIS, and/or led to believe in their radical mentalities in the UK. Women are often mis-looked by those who are attempting to understand the spread of influence terrorism has. In the documentary, Aisha went undercover and created a twitter account and tweeted radical messages in support of terrorist groups and their committed acts (Real Stories). Within a few months, she gained access to other women on twitter with the same ideology. She eventually met them face to face in secret meetings by invitation only where women preached on radical Islam (Real Stories). The way terrorism is spreading is by mouth to mouth and the gaining of trust of those who are targeting them.

In the past, the general blind hope among people was that our future is always intact. They believed that although terrorism did harm, children would never be hurt, or used to inflict pain on others. This is no longer, and has never been true. Sculpting the minds of the young is what will continue the belief in the doctrines of terrorism in the future. To think that everyone is safe is the first mistake. For every tragedy that happens with terrorism, parents might say to themselves that their children are too young to understand and should not know about the event. However, due to information being spread faster than ever before, children find out things they might not have in the past. They are misled now more than ever. This means that the world has to take action and not be comfortable to live in oblivion, now more than ever.

Works Cited

Abubakar, Aminu. "As Many as 200 Girls Abducted by Boko Haram, Nigerian Officials Say." *Africa*. CNN, 16 April 2014. Web. 5 July 2016.

Associated Press. and Louise Boyle. "Trial Hears how Boston Victim Martin Richard, 8, suffered 'Visceral Pain' Before He Died as Jury Decides if Dzhokhar Tsarnaev Should be Executed." *News*. Daily Mail, 23 April 2015. Web. 5 July 2016.

Bennhold, Katrin. "Jihad and Girl Power: How ISIS Lured 3 London Girls." *Europe*. The NewYork Times, 17 Aug. 2015. Web. 5 July 2016.

Boghani, Priyanka. "Why Afghanistan's Children are Used as Spies and Suicide Bombers."*Children of ISIS*. Frontline, 17 Nov. 2015. Web. 5 July 2016.

Counterterrorism Guide. "Boko Haram."

Terrorist Groups. National Counterterrorism

Center, n.d. Web. 26 June 2016.

Greenwald, Glenn. "What's Scarier:

Terrorism or Governments Blocking Websites in its

Name?" The Intercept, 17 Mar. 2015. Web. 14 July

2016.

History.com Staff. "Boston Marathon

Bombings." *History.com.* A+E Networks, 11 July

2016.Web. 26 June 2016.

Homeland Security Institute. "The Internet

as a Tool for Recruitment and Radicalization of the

Youth." 24 April 2009. PDF file. 14 July 2016.

Kaplan, Eben. "Terrorists and the Internet."

Publications. Council on Foreign Relations, 8 Jan.

2009. Web. 14 July 2016.

Morgan, Winsor. "Nigeria's Education Crisis: Boko Haram Targeting Schools." *World.* International Business Times, 2 Dec. 2015. Web. 26 June 2016.

Real Stories. "ISIS Women Unveiled (Terrorism Documentary) - Real Stories". Online Video Clip. YouTube. YouTube, July 14 2016. Web.8 August 2016.

Winter, Tom. "Date Set for Tsarnaev's Official Death Sentence in Boston Bombing." *Boston Bombing Trial.* NBC News, 25 June 2015. Web. 26 June 2016.

Chapter 7

Each Strand and Shade

Hair in different arrays of tangled curls, the skin color rainbow from tawny to ebony, and a history complicated and bittersweet, being black has a unique point of view that is different from other ethnicities, and their opinion of themselves has not always been positive, particularly among women. Lebogang Mashile, a South African poet who has a focus on young girls, writes to address the issues in black communities that no one wants to speak about, but many face the effects of that silence every day. *Tomorrow's Daughters* is a poem for black girls about confidence, not just through accepting one's physical features when others may ridicule it, but being fearless and united when empowered with a voice.

Tomorrow's Daughters is written in free verse, following a natural speech pattern that could not be given with a rhyme scheme. Mashile's purpose in doing this is to send a message to her audience. She even starts off with, "I want to tell you a poem", because she wants black girls to imagine her genuine voice coaxing them to have a voice, instead of merely giving the words a quick glance. However, what Mashile states in her poem is only half the message, implying that the confidence issue within black girls has its roots from a struggle between them and not always against a common enemy.

Colorism is discrimination within a race against darker skin tones (Nittle). This is a massive issue in black communities. Many women with darker skin go through life feeling inferior to those with lighter skin, and this way of thinking can even seep into their relationships. Black men who have dark skinned women in their family admit to refusing to date girls who were "too dark", ironically the same skin tone as them (Lamb). However, on the other side of the color spectrum, light skinned girls face difficulties as well. Darker girls accuse them of feeling superior and prettier, causing a divide. As a result, many light skinned girls are told they are not "black enough" (OWN). Mashile is not oblivious to this, using repetition in her poem, stating "Pretty black girls" three times (Mashile). She does not specify what skin tone one has to be in order to reach the standard of pretty because there is not one. She included all black girls, one of the many ways she is telling them to set aside their differences and focus on the real fight.

Variance in hair texture seems to be for many a minor issue; but it is actually as much of a sensitive topic as skin tones. The ideology for many is that the straighter one's curl is, the more attractive that girl is. Black girls resort to relaxers to get a uniformly straight look for a long amount of time. Many start young, and the process can actually be painful. The chemical sodium hydroxide is put on the hair to break down its protein causing it to become straight, and it has the potential of leaving the user with a burnt scalp (Fihlani). This is not to say that relaxer is the enemy, but it is the thought process behind many girls who are using it for the wrong reason. The poem calls for "Voices that curl the straight edges of history and hair thin slices of movement turning the world kinky" (Mashile). She uses personification to show black girls that the qualities of their hair they are so desperate to change should be something they are proud of, therefore proud of themselves and confident to change the world around them. She calls them to embrace their kinky and curly hair, and change how history taught them to see themselves.

These negative assumptions about what being black really implies have to start at some age. It seeps its way in, almost unconsciously. If one asked a black girl, even as young as five, how they know what the world thinks of them, they would shrug their tiny shoulders, not even knowing themselves. In the 1940's, a study was conducted by a psychologist Kenneth Clark, along with his wife Mary, called the Doll Test where they placed four dolls that were only different by race in front of children from three to seven, and asked them to pick

their color of race and they race that they liked

better (LDF). A majority of children picked the

white doll as their preference and gave it good

characteristics (LDF). Many could contradict on

how this research applies to the present, considering

how different things were in the past on

discrimination compared to now. However, in 2010,

the Doll Test resurfaced and was administered by

CNN on the show "AC360". Girls, as well as other

children, within this study pointed at the darkest

doll and stated she was bad and dumb because of

her dark skin (Billante, Jill, and Chuck Hadad). In a

line from *Tomorrow's Daughters*, the poem warns

of this: "Who [pretty black girls] don't relax and let

their dreams lie away" (Mashile). Mashile was

telling them not to settle for feeling ashamed of

themselves, and not to slacken the resolve that things should be different. However, even after decades they still feel the same way about themselves as their ancestors did before them.

Everything has an origin, a place where it all began. For black people, this is no different. The beliefs of changing their physical appearance to fit in their milieu, resigning themselves to being unworthy and the self-esteem issue worm its way into the minds of their children, all have roots from their days on the plantation. During this period in America's history, the slaves were categorized into the house slaves and field slaves (Thompson). Those in the field wrapped their natural hair up, keeping it hidden and the house slaves were required to look presentable by wearing wigs like their masters (Thompson). It is easy to see the slaves' train of thought: if white skin plus straight hair equals power and control, then if they looked more like who controlled them maybe they would never have been a slave. Hence, the inferior race should strive to look like the superior one. This was a mind game, a psychological way of controlling them by breaking down their confidence. This is what the poem was referring to when it stated, "I revere people to my own detriment / perhaps you did too" (Mashile). Black people actually began to believe what their masters were telling them, and strived to look like them, putting their looks on a pedestal. However, maybe surprising to some is that jealousy was at play in this by the white master. In the 1800s in Louisiana, the extravagant hairstyles of the black women were gathering attention from the white population (Cassandre). To protect their social class the Tigon Law was introduced that ordered all black women to cover their hair with a headdress, but they found a way to fight back by wearing the headdresses in interesting ways with appealing patterns (Cassandre).

Along the way, little rebellions like these popped up across the country leading up to the Black Power Movement of the 1960s (Chinwe). Black women were letting their hair out by sporting huge afros, and gaining long awaited pride. The movement caused awareness among black people to accept one another, and taught them how to be comfortable in their own skin. Wearing their hair natural had become a political statement. They were finally grasping what Mashile writes about, "How to look at their hearts / With eyes blaring at full blast" (Mashile).

The poem uses an allusion to Emily Dickinson to show how one does not have to be loud or obnoxious to make a change or gain confidence.

> I respect the disciplined silent screamers
>
> Who expose the holes
>
> Emily Dickinson, I am climbing through
>
> To your wooden shed of isolation
>
> (Mashile).

Dickinson was known as a recluse, but her work spoke for itself. Just like the women in the Black Power Movement wore their hair in silent rebellion, Mashile tells black girls to use any form of medium, loud or silent, with neither being the inferior to unite, and make an impact on the stagnant course of history. However, she calls them to change it together. Nowhere in her poem does it state pretty black girl. It was always in the plural sense, implying a united front, and she writes that they should wear "crowns of change" (Mashile). *Tomorrow's Daughters* is Mashile's heartfelt manner of not just telling, but pleading with black girls that with each strand of their braids, twists, curls, kinks, and shades of skin, use all their being to say something, do something… change everything.

Works Cited

Billante, Jill, and Chuck Hadad. "Study: White and black children biased toward lighter skin." *U.S.* CNN, 14 May 2010. Web. 17 Apr. 2016.

Cassandre. "Shocking History: Why Women of Color in the 1800s Were Banned From Wearing Their Hair In Public." *Culture*. Black Girl Long Hair, 7 July 2014. Web. 17 Apr. 2016.

Chinwe. "The Natural Hair Movement in the '60s and '70s; How It Began and Why It Ended." *Culture*. Black Girl Long Hair, 12 Jan. 2015. Web. 17 Apr. 2016.

Fihlani, Pumza. "Being African: What does hair have to do with it?" *News.* BBC, 22 July 2015.Web. 17 Apr. 2016.

Lamb, Taylor. "Light Skinned Girls and Colorism." *Issues.* My Black Matters, 25 Sept. 2015. Web. 17 Apr. 2016.

LDF. "Doctors Kenneth and Mamie Clark and "The Doll Test." *Brown at 60: The Doll Test.* NAACP, n.d. Web. 17 Apr. 2016.

Mashile, Lebogang. "TOMORROW'S DAUGHTERS." *Poems.* Lyrikline, n.d. Web. 17 Apr. 2016.

Nittle, Nadra. "Definition of Colorism." *Race Relations.* About News, 25 Nov. 2014. Web. 17 Apr. 2016.

OWN. "Colorism: Light-Skinned African-American Women Explain The Discrimination They Face." *HuffPost.* Huffington Post, 13 Jan. 2014. Web. 17 Apr. 2016.

Thompson, Cheryl. "Black Women and Identity: What's hair got to do with it?" *Michigan Feminist Studies.* Michigan Publishing, n.d. Web. 17 Apr. 2016.

www.ingramcontent.com/pod-product-compliance
Lightning Source LLC
Chambersburg PA
CBHW070214290526

45789CB00002B/986